MW01242513

"Through this book E given to us in Scriptu... ... concise doctrinal statements and ties them into practical application that can be used to help growing disciples develop a real-world theology as they mature in their faith. Pastors and teachers can use these chapters to help their disciples develop a biblically sound understanding of God's Word, the church, the sacraments and the work of salvation. This work will be an excellent tool for believers to use in their lives and in the lives of those they mentor in the faith."
- Rev. Steve Lawson Executive Director, Advent Christian General Conference

"If there is such a thing as Reformed Theology for Dummies, this is it. With skill and brevity, Erik lays out the essential truths of Christian faith and asks the questions that will bury those truths deep in your heart and mind. Theology doesn't have to be intimidating, not should it ever be shallow or oversimplified; this book manages to walk a tightrope. Mr. Reynolds' writing, saturated in Scripture, establishes each doctrine line upon line, precept upon precept, as all faithful Biblical teaching should."
- Rev. Luke Copeland Senior Pastor, Central Advent Christian Church

"This is a digest of systematic theology that is nevertheless substantive and will prove to be a valuable resource for discipling new believers in Christ. In addition Erik's work should provide a valuable introduction to the joy of "the study of God" (which is what theology means) that will encourage many to go even deeper, always relying on the source of sound theology, the Holy Scriptures. He is careful in each chapter to show the implications for how theology leads to doxology (the praise of God) and how theological engagement must impact one's life. "
-Rev. Lou Going Minister of Pastoral and Church Health, Maranatha Advent Christian Conference

Discover
Ancient Truths For Today

A Guide For The Church
(Book Two)
Erik B. Reynolds

To the body of Christ,

May God bless you by His Word and Spirit with teachers and shepherds who point you to Him so that you'd be equipped for every good work.

Thank you to my editors, proofreaders, and cover designer. You continue to be an incredible encouragement as this series of books for the church continue to unfold.

Table of Contents

Forward

Several years ago three young pastors met at a diner in northeast Rhode Island to get to know each other. If you have ever met Erik Reynolds, Tom Loghry, or myself, then you would probably guess that that hour long get-together for breakfast was anything but an hour long. Three hours later, and nearly lunchtime, we were forced to tear ourselves away from a deep conversation about theology. I had not met Erik Reynolds in person before that day, but realized immediately that our thinking was very much aligned, as was our passion for the truth of God's Word.

It has been a true joy these past six or so years to get to know Erik, to watch his faith and ministry grow, to sharpen his thinking even as he has sharpened my own. As Erik sought ordination, I had the honor to be part of his ordination council, seeing in a new way how seriously he takes the truth of Scripture as he engaged with the other pastors on that committee. And most of all, it has been a pleasure and a privilege to call Erik a friend and brother in Christ. But enough about Erik. This isn't about him. Rather, it is about a new resource Erik has written for the church: *Discover:Ancient Truths for Today.*

It has often been said that as followers of Christ we are called to "know God and make Him known." It is only possible to make something known, of course, if we first know it. Therefore, we study theology. Theology is, at its heart, a summary of what is taught in the Bible. The Bible is God's self-revelation to us, His creation. And that is what this book is all about. Who is God? Who are we? What is sin? How can we be saved? What is salvation? These crucial questions, and more, are all discussed herein.

The basis for *Discover* was a series of theological statements Erik assembled while seeking ordination. Though he did not have an extensive theological education, he has been motivated, by the work of the Holy Spirit, to study and discuss these theological truths from the scriptures and through the theological works of many men and women of faith. The fruit of this study is in your hands, as an introduction to Christian doctrine.

Erik provides for you here a revised version of those brief statements, but he does not stop there. This is not a dense, theological tome, but rather a clear, concise articulation of core biblical truths. Many are afraid to pick up a book on theology, or are overwhelmed once they do. But that should not be the case here. After laying out his brief explanation of each key doctrine, Erik has provided for us a down-to-earth explanation of it to help us grasp the basic concept, follows that explanation with discussion about how this teaching causes us to worship God in different ways, and then finishes each section with a series of questions that help us grasp and apply all that has been said.

So I commend this work to you. Read it. Study it. Answer the questions. Write out your own versions of the statements contained herein. But don't stop there. Share it and discuss with your brothers and sisters in Christ. Ask others who are older in the faith to refine your thinking, just as Erik has done. And use it as a guide to disciple those who are younger in their faith. May this book assist you in being a disciple and making disciples.

Rev. Nathaniel Bickford
Teaching Elder, Whitefield Christian Church
MAR, Theological and Historical studies, Westminster Theological Seminary
Soli Deo Gloria

Series Introduction

I began writing a guide to making disciples in every area of life back in 2017. It started off by offering practical ideas about how to open up your home, be intentional at work, and use your hobbies all as ways to make disciples. Why? The call to make disciples comes from Jesus and it is our purpose as Christians. However, this can seem like an incredibly daunting task when working 40 hours a week and running kids all over town for sports.

So in the first book I laid out a foundation for why to make disciples and ways to accomplish that end. This led into an effort to write a series of guides and books that will provide material as you take on the responsibility of fulfilling your Gospel call. These works are necessarily concise so that you can read them, wrestle with the ideas, and then put them into immediate practice. These works tend to be broad in scope and go to a depth that will spark interest as well as encourage you in the process.

Encouragement can often be lacking when we read Christian works. Why is that? I don't think it's the intent of the authors, but we can all too often feel as though we are never doing enough. We are quick to forget that Christ is enough and our call isn't to be Christ, but to proclaim Him. For that reason, I encourage you to make disciple-making a lifelong pursuit. Consider the Christian life a marathon and not a sprint. At times you will find that you begin to sprint in order to catch up and that's okay as long as you rely on Jesus as your source of this boost in energy and effort. When you self-will a sprint along this marathon you can find that you will become burnt out and left in depression because you'll never be where you want to be. Friend, you might not be where you want to be, but you're exactly where God has placed you. His grace is sufficient for you; embrace Him and His mercy. Learn the truth He reveals for your good and His glory.

Preface

Do we really need another book on introducing theology and doctrine? Yes, but this isn't it. There are numerous good books that properly articulate God's Word in summations called Doctrine. They defend doctrine, teach it, and are a blessing to God's people. In the Suggested Reading in the back of this book I include some of the best for you to read. One thing this work doesn't do is thoroughly defend each truth and engage with opposing views, which the works listed in the back do very well!

The intent of Discover: Ancient Truths For Today is to provide a resource to God's people that walks them through some of the most important truths of Scripture, explaining how they lead to worship and action.

The approach taken in this work is to articulate truths that are critical to the life of God's people and to show how they relate to our worship of God and how they stir us into action.

My last book Go! Teaching all that Jesus commands to those Jesus commands us to reach intended to teach and give practical ideas on how you can make disciples in every single part of your life. It took the reader through the process of inventorying their lives and assessing how they can leverage what they are already doing in order to point others to Christ and encourage growth in Him. That work raises another question, "what are you to teach?". Stay! Is exactly the type of resource you can use to begin instructing others in what Christ teaches. Start by reading this resource by yourself and take ownership of the faith. Then read this book with someone else, a Small Group, a Sunday School Class, or a Bible Study.

I encourage you to critically read the doctrinal statements in the beginning of each chapter. How might you word things differently? You should read the associated Scriptures and assess my accuracy. When studying with another person or in a group you could each write your own statement on each doctrine based on Scripture and discuss it. God's Word is meant to be read, studied, and engaged with. You should prayerfully read His Word, but also interact with it through discussing within a community. This has actually been a quite common practice within the church since its founding in the first century.

The most important thing is that you are seeking God, treasuring His truths by worship, and applying His truths to your life. This, of course, includes sharing those truths with others. You should be sharing these truths in all of life. Your study of theology doesn't end once you leave the church facility or exit your home. You put into practice these ancient and wonderful truths in the workplace, school, supermarket, and sporting events. Theology affects your outlook on life and shapes your worldview.

Several years ago I was attending a large church with all the glitz and glam of a Rock Concert. The pastor said that the intent of this particular church wasn't to study or discuss theology and doctrine, it was to see people come to know Christ. There is something admirable in his sincere desire to see people come to know the Lord. However, something struck me as "off." I said to my wife, "Didn't he just reveal a certain aspect of his own theology, that theology doesn't matter?" Theology is the study of God, but is also a term that we use as an umbrella under which all other doctrines, or "ologies," sit.

The reason that theology is so important is because God gave us His Word in the Scriptures. God says something and His people need to listen. Not only should we listen to what God says, but also study His Word. Not only should we study it, but also learn it. In the Great Commission Jesus calls His disciples to "teach all that I have commanded." How can we teach all that the Lord commands if we don't know what He says? It's like what pastor and theologian Voddie Baucham says, *"The modern church is producing passionate people with empty heads who love the Jesus they don't know very well."*

Engaging in the study of God's Word and what it teaches will lead you to greater worship of Jesus so that you're not empty headed and your passion for God is properly directed. This study will make you a stronger disciple and in turn God's church will be made stronger.

The first part of each chapter lays out a particular doctrine that is important to the Christian faith and needed within the life of the believer. Then we will move to how this doctrine leads to doxology, which is the worship of God. Lastly, the chapter will include what this doctrine demands us to do, where we will explore the practical application of the doctrine.

All too often we can let the study of God's Word and the doctrines of Scripture intimidate us and believe that the deep things of God are inaccessible for God's people. This couldn't be further from the truth. You need to know what God teaches as much as your pastor does, and you need to help others learn from the Scriptures as well. Doctrine might seem largely philosophical on the surface, but it's actually quite practical.

How are theology and doctrine practical? When we learn about God and what He says it affects our hearts and how we feel about God. Our relationship to God is in one way objective - based on the work of Christ - - and subjective - experiential in that we "taste and see" the goodness of God. God's truth stirs in us an affection for Him that leads to worship and praise. This stirring affection elicited by truth, or *Doctrine*, also calls us to obedience. Obedience is simply believing what God says and following it. The authority of Scripture should cause us to study it intently. As we study it we obey it, because it's the very Word of God, whom we love deeply. Take for instance the following examples of right doctrine leading to right practice (obedience):

- The doctrine of the church (Ecclesiology) causes us to join a local community and be active participants.
- The nature of man (Anthropology) causes us to better understand the evil in our world and recognize that the antidote is the cross.
- The nature of sin (Hamartiology) causes us to examine our hearts and leads to repentance.
- The doctrine of grace and mercy causes us to be merciful and patient with people.

- God's love towards us creates in us a love for others.

You will find that each chapter has two sections. One is labeled *Doctrinal Statement* and the other *Doxology and Application*. *Doctrinal Statement* is exactly that - a theological statement that sums up a particular truth that the Scriptures teach. I do not spend time defending this truth though I include Scripture references for you to look up and consider. If you are looking for a more thorough treatment of these doctrines I encourage you to look in the *Appendix* for greater theological works.

Doxology and Application is a section in which I seek to unfold for you how this particular doctrine leads to right praise of God and right application in life. The two are necessarily intertwined because praise leads to application as much as application leads to praise. Who is to be praised? God! Some doctrines are more easily applied in the everyday life of the Christian and the church. Other doctrines might be rightly applied in how they lead us in worship. Why is this? The Scriptures are first and foremost the story of God redeeming a people from their fallenness and rebellion. Therefore, we must first come to the right understanding of God, Creation, and redemption so that we will praise Him forevermore.

May God bless your study by pointing you to the Lord Jesus Christ and finding joy in Him.

Authority and Authorship of Scripture

Doctrinal Statement

The Bible is authoritative and sufficient in all matters of faith and practice (Ps. 119:160). It is God's special revelation of Himself to man, revealing His holiness, man's sinfulness, the redemption of man and the world, and the story of His people. It should be used for teaching, correction, preaching, and training (2 Tim. 3:16). The original manuscripts are without error and were inspired by the Holy Spirit as He provided exact words for the human author while allowing for that author's particular writing style and personality to shine through. (Tit. 1:2; 2 Sam. 7:28; Prov. 30:52; 2 Pet. 1:20-21).

Doxology and Application

There are two kinds of revelation, general and special. General revelation is God's disclosure of Himself through creation. We see this in Romans 1:19-21, *"For what can be known about God is plain to them, because God has shown it to them. For his invisible attributes, namely, his eternal power and divine nature, have been clearly perceived, ever since the creation of the world, in the things that have been made. So they are without excuse. For although they knew God, they did not honor him as God or give thanks to him, but they became futile in their thinking, and their foolish hearts were darkened."*

General revelation reveals God's presence and glory to the world. As the world rejects that presence and glory, they condemn themselves due to their unbelief in their holy Creator (John 3:18). Praise be to God who gave us His Word, which we call special revelation. This Word that we call the Bible leads us into a saving knowledge of God that general revelation is unable to do.

God authored Scripture through the Holy Spirit and by the hand of man. He perfectly spoke to His people by inspiring human authors to write down His words.

The Bible is the Christian's measure of faith and practice because it reveals the will of God in the world, which is for us to believe in Jesus Christ. It is the work of Jesus that has already saved, but the Scriptures reveal that work to man in the present. The Bible also reveals to man God's desire to be worshipped, invites them into His mission of glorifying His name, and exposes the fallenness of the world. It is upon this doctrine of the Scriptures that we can confidently build all other doctrines.

God has given to the church preachers and teachers of the Word to equip the saints for ministry (Eph. 4:11). What are they to equip the saints with? The Word of God. It is through the Word that He orders His church, instructs us in baptism and The Lord's Supper, and reveals salvation. If Christ is the solid rock, then the Word of God through the illumination and instruction of the Holy Spirit gives us the ability to see that rock.

How good is God that He would reveal Himself in this way? He provides for us the means to know Him. We don't simply have an oral tradition of ethics, but a written down account of God's work and Word so that we can know Him intimately. We have a God who desires to be known and who knows us. This should create a sense of gratitude among His people as they experience the grace and grandeur found in His Word.

Having received this priceless gift, what should we do, but read and reread, memorize, and study each word, sentence, and thought, we are likewise called to engage with great enthusiasm the Word of God. We have a lifetime of getting to know God more, but it's not something that we should put off. Why might that be? The Creator of the universe, who has purchased you with His own blood, means to communicate with you and that means of communication has been enclosed in the Bible. The Bible is a gift to us from God.

Consider how you are currently engaging with God's Word. Are you reading it on your own? How about with friends? Is the only time you're engaging with God's Word when the pastor preaches on Sunday mornings? I've heard many dear brothers and sisters say that they are waiting for God to speak to them. What a glorious, holy, and righteous request to make! To hear from God you must first open up your Bible and read His Word prayerfully and with careful study.

To better appreciate the blessings of God's Word I highly recommend A.W. Pink's *Profiting From The Word*. The Word of God is profitable for teaching and instruction. Praise God for such a bountiful treasure!

Study Questions:

1. What does the Bible say about itself?
2. Why is God's Word important?
3. How can you commit to spending more time reading and studying Scripture?
4. Is your worldview, which is simply the lens in which you see everything, shaped by the Bible?

Use the space that remains to write out what you believe about the Word of God.

The Being of God

Doctrinal Statement

There is only one true God (Deu. 6:4; 1 Tim. 2:5),
eternally existent in three persons who act in
accordance with one divine will (John 5:19; 8:28;
12:49; 14:10). Each person of the Trinity has a distinct
relationship and role (John 1:18; 3:16; 14:26; 16:7) and
is equal in authority and power (1 Cor. 8:6; John
5:21-23; Matt. 12:31) with the other persons.

God the Father is the One Who watches over His
people (Ex. 4:22) and who sent Jesus as the Savior into
the world (1 Jn. 4:14). Through faith in Jesus, believers
are adopted into the family of God (Eph. 1:5). The
Father is the one who chose a people to give to His Son
since before the foundation of the world (Jn. 17; Rm.
8:29-30).

God the Son, like the other persons of the Trinity, has
existed eternally (John 1:1; Col. 1:17) and is spoken of
in Old Testament prophecy (Gen. 3:15). Jesus is truly
man (Heb. 2:14) and truly God (Jn. 1:18; Lk. 3:22). He
was born of a virgin (Isa. 7:14; Matt. 1:23), lived a
sinless life (Heb 4:15), died on the cross as the penal
substitutionary atonement for man's sin (Matt. 6:12),

rose from the dead (Lk. 24:6), ascended into heaven (Acts 1:9), and is coming again in glory (1 Co. 15).

God the Holy Spirit is the one whom Jesus sent as a helper that indwells all believers. He teaches (Jn. 14:26) and leads (Jn. 16:13) Christ-followers (Jn. 14:16). The Spirit convicts of sin (Jn. 16:8), intercedes for (Rom. 8:26) those who believe, and regenerates (Tit. 3:5) those whom the Father has chosen so that they will respond in faith and repentance, believing the Gospel of Jesus Christ. It is in cooperation with the Holy Spirit that believers can better understand and study God's Word (Jn. 14:26). The Holy Spirit endows believers with specific gifts to serve God (1 Cor. 12:11) and serve the church (Eph. 4:11-13).

Doxology and Application

I once had someone ask me to recommend a book on prayer. I pointed them to a wonderful and helpful book by Paul E. Miller, *A Praying Life.* Paul gives a good theological and biblical understanding of prayer and accompanies it with some tremendous tools to aid the believer in practicing God-honoring and personally vibrant prayer. However, I wish I had accompanied that book with the following advice, *learn who God is.*

Prayer at its most fundamental level is the application of our communion with God; it is interactive in that we declare God's goodness and He makes His presence more known to us. His presence brings us joy, hope, comfort, strength, peace, and more. The first part, our declaration to God of His goodness is only possible and effective to the extent to which we understand His goodness. Therefore, we must know God as intimately, truthfully, and accurately as possible.

We can often think of prayer as a list of demands or requests directed to God on behalf of ourselves and others. This is good. Jesus tells us to bring our petitions to Him. He tells us to direct our prayers to the Father and make our petitions in His name. Jesus also promises that the Spirit will guide us. These are theological statements about how we view the will of God, His nature, and His desire for us to communicate with Him. In reading the Psalms along with prayers in both the Old and New Testament, we can also see a picture of a vibrant prayer life, one in which God's people focus much of their prayer on the nature and character of God.

To understand Jesus' teaching on prayer we must understand God's Trinitarian nature: He is coexistent and coeternal as one essence, and exists as three persons. All three persons of God have the same will, purpose, character, and all other traits. Each person has a unique ministry and their own distinctions. The Son died as the Savior, The Father calls the saved, and the Spirit applies salvation and regenerates the sinner as they become a saint.

God is infinite. We should spend our lives getting to know Him more in the same way we get to know our spouse for the rest of our lives. Study, learn, apply! The process is unending and it may seem daunting if you treat God like a subject to learn in school. Instead we should look at this learning as a privilege as much as a responsibility. As we learn more about God's nature, His character, and His attributes our worship will taste sweeter. It will flow out of our awe-inspired hearts like an underwater spring. This worship is found in prayer and is often demonstrated communally as we worship together as the church.

Lastly, I'd like you to consider how God's uniqueness should quiet our souls and create a humility within us. God is the one whom we have sinned against. He is the Creator and unlike any other being in the universe. When we gaze upon the glorious nature of God the center of our world is shifted from ourselves to Him. It is all too easy for us to get caught up in ourselves. We become our own masters who serve ourselves and expect others to do the same. When there is conflict within our souls, homes, or churches it is most often due to this perspective being lost—life is centered on God; when it isn't we can only expect dysfunction.

So the next time you are feeling anxious, think about who God is and meditate on His sovereignty in your life. When people are arguing in your church over music or carpet color, remember that God is the one we serve, not ourselves. In fact it is with a correct and worshipful view of God that Paul can easily teach that we are to count others as more important than ourselves. Their good is more important than my good, because God is supreme and He has called me to serve rather than be served.

Study Questions

1. How would you describe God?
2. What passages of Scripture come to mind when you think about God's nature?
3. What areas of your life are influenced by a proper view of God?
4. Can you think of a time when humility in light of God's nature could have caused you to handle a difficult situation differently?

Use the space that remains to write out what you believe about the being of God.

The Church

The universal church, or body of Christ, includes all who have faith in Jesus as their Lord and Savior (1 Pet. 2:5; Eph. 2:19-22). Though all who put their faith in Jesus are united as one body, it is the local group of believers who constitute the local church or congregation (Acts 5:11-14). The local church is responsible for sound teaching (Acts 6:3-6), fellowship (Acts 2:42), evangelism (Mk. 16:15; Acts 13:47), discipleship (1 Pet. 5:1-4), and discipline (Matt. 18:15-20). This local church is responsible for administering two ordinances: the Lord's Supper (Matt. 26:26-30) and believer's Baptism (Matt. 28:19). The Body of Christ has members and leaders, who are called elders (Eph. 4:11) and deacons (Acts 6) and who care for the church spiritually and physically. The leaders of a local church are responsible for the congregation's well being and the members are responsible for how they respond to leadership (Heb. 13:17).

Doxology and Application

God promises His people that He will manifest His glory in their lives. This is exciting as much as it is overwhelming. You might say, "The Creator of all things manifests His glory in my life?" But of course He does! In John 17:14-19 Jesus prays to the Father on behalf of His disciples. This prayer is quite telling as He says *"I have given them your word, and the world has hated them because they are not of the world,"* He would go on to ask God to keep them in the world. In fact it's for the world's sake that God keeps His people in the world. Why? To make Him known to the world.

Manifesting God's glory in the world is to point those outside of the Kingdom to the King of Kings. God's people do this by preaching the Gospel, demonstrating love for one another, and showing love to the world. Caring for a sick neighbor demonstrates God's love and manifests His glory to the nations as you serve your neighbor in the name of Christ without the expectation of reward. In the midst of your servitude you extend the Gospel call and point to the one who sent you: God.

Anyone can serve the poor and broken-hearted. In fact it's looked upon as virtuous in today's society. The Christian, however, serves not to feel good because they've done a good deed, but instead serves out of love for God and neighbor. The love of God and service to Him is the motivator to serve our neighbor or sister in Christ. Thomas Manton puts it this way, *"It is one thing to do good work for the glory of God, another to do them for the glory of ourselves. We may do good works to be seen in the first respect, but not the last."* So the church works together to glorify God, not themselves.

You might be asking what in the world this has to do with the doctrine of the church. The church is God's people, it isn't a building or a place. Though a church gathers regularly in a geographical location, it isn't the facility in which it meets. You can be a church without a building but you can't be a church without the people of God. The people of God—the church, are the ones who are collectively responsible for making God's glory manifest on Earth. To be in the faith and outside of the church is antithetical—they are opposing forces. Think of it like a magnet. The local church is a magnet that holds you in place so that you remain in proper relationship with God.

God has given you the gift of community. This community is where you are to serve others, care for your fellow believers, carry out God's mission, disciple one another, worship, be baptized, celebrate communion, study the Word and hear it taught, receive counsel, and find accountability. In fact the local church is God's expression of Heaven on Earth. Throughout eternity we will be worshiping with the Universal Church unaffected by sin and away from the fallenness of this world. Presently we experience a taste of this heavenly peace in the gathering of God's people.

Individually we are responsible for carrying out God's mission in our daily lives as much as we are responsible for supporting the church's efforts in carrying out that same mission. So we make God's name manifest on Earth, as mentioned above, by serving our neighbor in His name.

In the same way we make God's presence manifest on Earth by supporting our local church through regular weekly worship, participating in its ministries, making ourselves available to serve, and by being served. We are called to set aside our own ambitions, preferences, and animosities in favor of caring for our brothers and sisters in Christ. We are to mutually submit to one another and work for the good of our fellow believers. There is no greater picture of this than Acts 2:42-47 where the church met daily to pray, study, eat, worship, and care for each other's physical needs.

How great and gracious is our God? He gives us one another to spur us on in the faith. He knows that the life to which He has called us is difficult. It is an arduous and daunting task to point the world to Christ, so He gives us the church, God's people. Not only are we accompanied by God who carries us on in this holy mission, but we have fellow believers to care, love, strengthen, encourage, and admonish us. What's God's plan when we start acting sideways? He's given us brothers in Christ to tenderly reveal our sin and lovingly point us to the Gospel. What's God's plan when we are discouraged because of a tragic life circumstance? He's given us sisters in Christ to pray with and point us to the hope we have in Christ Jesus. What's God's plan when we realize how weak we are? He's given us brothers in Christ to remind us that our weakness is a gift so that we will be more apt to rely upon the Holy Spirit who indwells us.

God has equipped you for every good work. He is all powerful and calls His people together to manifest that power. What is His power able to do? Jesus says, *"the gates of Hell shall not prevail against it"* (Mt. 16:18), referring to God's church. Why is that? God protects His people as they go along in their mission. He gives them everything they need to carry out His will and purpose. This realization should evoke in us a deep joy and sense of peace. God surrounds us with His protection, which is found in His church.

Study Questions

1. Why has God established the church?
2. Can you think of a passage in Scripture that points to a function of the church?
3. How have you functioned as a church member?
4. What can you do to help your church function in a way that serves God and the community?

Use the space that remains to write out what you believe about the church.

Church Government

Doctrinal Statement

Jesus is the head of the church (Col. 1:18) and has entrusted earthly responsibility to undershepherds in caring for His church. There are two church offices mentioned in the New Testament:

Elders lead the local church by caring for the spiritual needs of the congregation (Eph. 4:11; 1 Timothy 3:2; 5:17; Tit. 1:9). The term "elder" can often be synonymous with pastor, shepherd, and overseer. Though these are likely aspects or different parts of the role of elder. The role of elder is served by men who are called, equipped, morally qualified (1 Tim. 2:9-15; 3:1-7; Tit. 1:5-9).

Deacons lead the local church by caring for the physical needs of the congregation (Acts 6:1-6). Qualifications of this office are found in 1 Timothy 3 and are served by both men and women.

Doxology and Application

When one comes into the faith they do so by the grace of God. He is their Lord, Savior, Creator, and so much more. He is also the head of the church. I remember a time when I had first come into the faith and I was having a discussion with a brother in Christ about who the church belongs to. Their position was that the church belongs to the pastor. I believed that the church belonged to the congregation. This conversation highlighted our shared ignorance and misunderstanding of what God says about His church. It belongs to Him and He has appointed Christ as its head.

The Apostle Paul writes, *"For the husband is the head of the wife even as Christ is the head of the church, his body, and is himself its Savior"* (Eph. 5:23). He is the one who has purchased the church by His blood. He leads, and cares for it. His current place is in heaven at the right hand of the Father. He is actively praying for His people, interceding on their behalf. Because He is no longer physically present with us, He raises up elders and deacons to care for His people.

Think of it like a young prince who through the death of his father inherits a Kingdom while he is still only a child. The father leaves instruction for an overseer to take charge of raising their child, caring for the kingdom, and leading through the daily work of the royal family. We are the royal family of God. We've been adopted into this family and will inherit the Kingdom of God. We are all infants awaiting our King's return. Until the time of His return, He has assigned leaders to the church who lead spiritually and physically. The New Testament calls these leaders elders and deacons.

Elder is a term used for men who are called and equipped by God to prayer and ministry of the Word (Acts 6:4). They can serve in different roles based on their calling and gifting as we see in Ephesians 4:11-12, "*And he gave the apostles, the prophets, the evangelists, the shepherds and teachers, to equip the saints for the work of ministry, for building up the body of Christ.*" So these men are a gift to the church for its building up in the faith. What does it mean to be built up in the faith? We grow individually and collectively as we move from spiritual milk to meat. We grow in our understanding of the Gospel, God's grace, and our application of what we believe.

So the elder leads by their ministry of the Word. This typically finds its application in preaching, teaching, disciple making, and searching the Scriptures and the will of God in their efforts to lead the people of God.

How should we structure the church budget? Is it time to hire an associate pastor or administrative assistant? What counsel shall we offer a church member who has been abandoned by their spouse? The elders should be outlining spiritual priorities for their local congregation and caring for their spiritual needs both proactively and reactively. When a church member is going through a spiritual crisis or needs help discerning the Scriptures, their elder(s) are eager to help.

Deacons on the other hand are men and women who serve the body of Christ by tending to their physical needs. They are the ones who often prepare the elements for communion, work on the church budget line items, care for the church facility, and disburse benevolence funds. When you read Acts 6 in its entirety you see that the purpose and blessing of a deacon is to free up the elders to minister the Word, by caring for the practical physical needs of the congregation.

So how does this work out in the context of the local church? Imagine the elders after having spent months in prayer and discussion conclude the church's ministries are misaligned. They realize that they are spending too much time and energy on fellowship activities and have neglected service to their community. They decide that it's time to cancel the weekly church luncheon in favor of doing it quarterly. Instead they are looking to put teams of church members together who will deliver fresh bread to the neighborhoods within five miles of the church facility.

The elders consult with the deacons to get their thoughts in practical matters in addition to those from the congregation. The deacons agree that this is a wonderful idea and had actually been praying about how they could be more outwardly focused. The deacons look to allocate funds from the church budget and coordinate the bakers and the teams. They map out which neighborhoods and what days, and get all of the elements together. The elders and deacons work together to provide some training for all participants in having Gospel focused conversations with those in the neighborhoods. This is a perfect example of how the two Biblical offices work together to carry out God's mission and care for His people.

There is great diversity in how churches are set up. Some have administrative boards, take their lead from the pastor, or see deacons fill both roles. No matter the current structure of your church, God has given to you leaders to equip you for the work of ministry. This is one way that God displays His love for His people. He not only leaves you a heavenly inheritance, but gives you people to care for you until that inheritance is fully realized.

Study Questions

1. Describe the difference between elders and deacons.
2. Why has God given the church elders and deacons?
3. What is your responsibility in regards to elders and deacons?
4. How do elders and deacons work together in leading God's church?

Use the space that remains to write out what you believe about the church government.

Baptism

Doctrinal Statement

Believer's baptism is a visible act that points to the Gospel. It is an act of obedience of a disciple who is identifying themself with the life, death, and resurrection of Jesus after confessing Him as Lord and Savior. Baptism by immersion into water and in the name of the Father, and the Son, and of the Holy Spirit, is the most accurate method of baptism found in the New Testament. (Mt. 28:19-20; Rom. 6:3-5; Acts 8:38-39)

Doxology and Application

God's people in the Old Testament were given a visible sign to symbolize His saving grace and their identification as His people. This gift to Israel was circumcision. God's people today, the church, are given the gift of baptism to identify them as followers of Jesus and to help them remember the grace of God's work in our salvation. Baptism has replaced circumcision as a sign of God's promise.

As a society we often look to the graduation ceremony as a rite of passage that signifies the accomplishment of a student and the faculty. A person graduates from high school and college based on their academic work and achievement. This includes likely hundreds if not thousands of assignments, which are graded by a teacher or professor. These grades are then given to another department that tracks the student's progress and when enough credits are attained they have completed the graduation requirements. The ceremony is the capstone event that signifies all of the hard work accomplished.

Baptism is the capstone act in the life of a follower of Jesus wherein the church recognizes the work of Christ in the person. It is something that is looked back upon by the disciple throughout their life as a time when they signaled to the world that they are no longer a servant of evil, but of light and life. They serve the King Most High, because He has saved them from the wretchedness of this world. No matter where God takes you in life you can always look back on the day you were baptized as a promise from God that you belong to Him. This of course differs from graduation in that the work celebrated isn't that achieved by the one being baptized, but Christ. In fact we celebrate an alien work done to an individual, which is a far greater accomplishment than endless Science experiments and English assignments.

The work of Christ is absolute. He was beaten, mocked and crucified after having lived a sinless life on Earth. This was done as God condescended Himself by taking on flesh in the Son. Baptism remembers this work and stands as a continual reminder of God's work, grace, and mercy. This isn't some throw away act or activity that should be done irreverently. It is something that should normally be done in the context of the local church so that the people of God can celebrate along with the person being baptized. It is an act wherein our lives should be put on pause so that we can be reminded that not only has this person been washed by the blood of Jesus, but so have I. Baptism is an act of worship and obedience that displays the glory of God in a way that nothing else does. It is truly a gift to the church communally and individually.

We are led into the waters of baptism in the same way that we are led into faith and repentance, by the Spirit. He comes upon us, changes our hearts so that we repent of our sin and believe in Christ. In a similar way, the Holy Spirit brings us into these waters and displays to us and all present the magnificence of God. It leads to right and proper worship as we submit to His call given to us through Peter to *"repent and be baptized"* (Acts 2:38). Our God doesn't leave us without markers, signs, or encouragement. He provides for our every need in this life and the next.

I once had a brother in Christ who came to me concerned for his salvation. He asked whether or not one can truly know whether they are saved or deceived. I pointed him to his baptism. "Did you have fruit of repentance in your life then and now?" I asked. "Yes!" He exclaimed. "Since then have you seen others come to Christ in the midst of your ministry?" He had.

This brother has all the elements of a follower of Jesus. His life was marked by the fruit of the Spirit, he daily repented of his sin, he loved Jesus, and made disciples at a number of churches. I shared with him that his baptism was a sign of the promise that God made to him that he was saved by the grace and mercy of our Lord. He wasn't saved by his works or even the evidence of faith, he was saved solely on the work of Christ and his faith in Him. However, these were all signs of fruit in his life that are promised in the life of a follower of Jesus.

God what a great gift you have given to us in the form of our baptism. May we always remember what your Son accomplished for us and the signs you've given to keep Him at the center of our lives.

Study Questions

1. Explain the purpose of baptism in your own words.
2. What does the New Testament teach about baptism?
3. What was your baptism like?
4. How could you support baptisms in your church more?

Use the space that remains to write out what you believe about baptism.

Communion

Doctrinal Statement

Communion or the Lord's Supper is a visible act that points to the Gospel. It includes bread, representing the broken body of Christ. Wine or grape juice represents the shed blood of Jesus, and is a sign of the New Covenant sealed with His blood. God gave Communion to the church in order to help us remember Jesus' death, affirm the faith, and physically commemorate the Gospel of Christ, which frees the body from the bondage of sin. (Mt. 26:26-27; 1 Cor. 10:16-17; 11:23-26)

Doxology and Application

There are two visible signs or representations of the Gospel that God has given the church, baptism and Communion. We have already discussed the first and now it's time for the second.

There are hundreds of thousands of portraits and paintings, maybe more, that seek to depict God, specifically Jesus.

- The Father is often portrayed in human form, even though He is Spirit.
- The Son is often pictured as a white anglo man, even though He was a First Century Jew.
- The Holy Spirit is illustrated as a dove, even though He only descended *like* a dove.

These man made depictions remind us that our hearts desire to worship something that is physically tangible or at least see a physical object as a representation of God. We think that it helps instruct us, lead us in worship, and make us feel like we know God more deeply.

We see many storybook Bibles, cartoons, curriculum, and movies catered to children as a way of instruction. Not everyone views the Second Commandment in exactly the same way, but we should at least consider how this instruction from God could better guide us in right worship and warn us against idolatry or wrong worship. It is revealing that many Christians lack any kind of zeal for baptism and Communion, which are given to us by God as physical reminders of His work in redemption and His presence with His people.

Communion is a gift given to the church so that she might be reminded of God's grace and mercy in Jesus Christ. The bread represents Jesus' body, which He took on physically at the incarnation, humiliating Himself, enduring all of the physical trials of a human. He was beaten and mocked, and suffered a gruesome and torturous death. The wine is given to God's people to remind them that their salvation and covenant with God is sealed by the shedding of Christ's blood, an allusion to and fulfillment of the Passover Lamb instituted in the Old Testament.

The Lord's Supper brings us to a place in which we reflect on a couple of things. First, we reflect on our need for Christ. Second, we reflect on the grace and mercy of God. Our remembrance of our need for Christ brings us to a place of sincere repentance and sorrow over our sin. We are reminded that our sin drove the nails into Christ. Without Him we would be the just recipients of God's wrath that is due all who rebel against their Creator. Jesus' punishment is our own, we have been crucified with Him. Instead of being crucified ourselves, He bears that wrath in our place by being *made sin who knew no sin* (2 Cor. 5:21a).

When we reflect upon the mercy of God we are driven to worship. We have been cleansed by Christ, He was made sin so that, *we would be made the righteousness of God* (2 Cor. 5:21b). This is called an alien righteousness, it is found outside of ourselves and given to us by God. Communion reminds us of this great exchange, Our perfect forgiveness, found in Jesus, is both complete and everlasting.

So as we meditate on the meaning of these elements we are drawn to God and are made more aware of His presence. This is a gift given to His people that expresses our Communion with Him and with one another. It is why Paul instructs the church to take Communion within the gathering of the saints. This idea of community is so central to communion that he suggests we wait until everyone is present before we partake (1 Cor. 11:33). It is also something that should be done with a clear conscience by believers only (1 Cor. 11:27-29).

This gift from the Lord drives us to Him. Communion and baptism should satisfy our desires for the physical worship of God as these are the means by which He desires to be worshipped along with the gathering of the saints as the Word is prayed, sung, and preached. He gives His people all that they need for right and true worship of Himself.

Your church and pastor may have some simple instructions regarding Communion. Here is a summary of what I laid out above, but in clearer terms. Communion should be done within the gathering of the church—that could be in special services or in the regular weekly gathering, but the emphasis is on it happening where all members who are believers are encouraged to partake. Our hearts should be examined prior to and in the midst of the distribution of the elements. Is there any unrepentant sin in my heart? If so, Paul says to go to the cross and seek forgiveness. Have I anything against a fellow believer? Go to them immediately and reconcile. Am I simply partaking in Communion because my family is doing it, or am I partaking because I am a redeemed follower of Jesus?

God gave us Communion so that we might remember Christ in His work and His grace. For that reason it drives us to a joyous state of being wherein Jesus is treasured above all things. His blood has been shed for us so that we'd be forgiven and united to Him as brothers and co-heirs of the Kingdom of God. What greater inheritance can one have than a Kingdom that cannot be overcome? We have countless promises from God and we are given the ordinances as a way to remind and point us to those promises. Praise God!

Study Questions

1. What is Communion?
2. How should you approach Communion.
3. Why does the church celebrate Communion and who can partake?
4. How does Communion encourage and sustain you in the faith?

Use the space that remains to write out what you believe about Communion.

God's Mission

God has a mission and His mission forms a church. God's mission is to call men and women to believe in Jesus, display His glory, and glorify Him forever (Ex. 14:4; Isa. 43:6-7; Jn. 20:21; Rom. 8:3;1Jn. 4:9). To that end the church's primary task is to make disciples of its neighbors, coworkers, family members, and the nations (Mt. 28:16-20, Acts 1:8).

Doxology and Application

Everyone wonders, "what is the meaning of life?" It has been the cause of countless books, movies, and plays. At the center of all human consciousness is the age old question, "what am I here for?" Someone once told me that the purpose of life is to pay taxes and die. This was prior to my belief in Christ and I thought to myself, "If that's it then what's the point in anything?" Such a nihilistic perspective can paralyze us as we consider the futility of life and come to the realization that without God there is very little point to it.

God has created all things. He owns every mountain and pebble, ocean and puddle, nation and person. He exercises dominion, reigns sovereignly, and works towards His own ends. His plans are never thwarted and He's always in control of every situation. His purpose is His own glory, meaning that His name, honor, majesty, beauty, and presence are to be made known in His creation. The pinnacle of His creation is man, whom He made in His own image. It is through man that He makes His glory known, but not all men. Though we learn that God's perfect glory will be unveiled to all in the New Heavens and New Earth, only those who have confessed and believed in Christ in this life will inherit this treasure. Those who have rejected God stand condemned and will perish. So the mission of the church is to make God's name known among the nations.

God has given all who call Him Lord a purpose in this life. There is no amount of science or secular philosophy that can satisfy man's thirst for meaning, only God can. He quenches this thirst by giving His people their mission, which is to serve Him. He has given us not only physical and spiritual life, but the answer to the most important question that each of us asks.

This is a display of God's goodness— that He allows us to be partakers in His glory, mission, and people. When we embrace God's mission we are in fact embracing God as He hands over to us the important and perpetual mission of sharing the precious gift of Christ with the world. God's mission to us comes by way of the cross and is as simple as bringing others to that same cross that has given us eternal life.

You can understand our mission as bringing Christ to people and then revealing to them the work of Christ. What could be more important or life giving than that? This causes all personal priorities to pale in comparison to the supremacy of the Gospel call. It is no small achievement to invent a new medical treatment, rise the corporate ladder, or make a difference in a child's life as a teacher, but such accomplishments are nothing compared to bringing a patient, coworker, or student to the Saviour. Medical treatments, career advancements, and teaching awards will pass away. Those works will burn up in the end, but the mission of God lasts for eternity. God is truly awesome!

So how might this practically work? How do you and I carry out this holy duty? First and foremost you must believe in Christ. Then you take others along for the ride with you. My previous book walked through the process of making disciples and that's really what this all boils down to. You can begin by inventorying your life and see where God has placed you to make disciples. You can create relationships in your workplace, with your hobbies, and in your neighborhood. Then you look to establish in these relationships a way to share Christ with them.

As a church we should be working to this same end. Our ministries should be focused on the mission of God, which is to make disciples. Most churches are a little off kilter because they either lean towards evangelizing the lost or towards discipling the saints. Instead we need to focus on both. We should be looking towards making disciples in all areas of life, which means we seek to proclaim the Gospel to the lost just as much as we grow in the Gospel within the people of God.

Therefore, you can look to what your church is currently doing. Are there ministries that are explicitly focused on proclaiming the Gospel? If so, see how you can be involved. If not, talk with your leadership to see how you can help out. As a pastor my dream is for someone to come up and say, "We need to be proclaiming the Gospel in the community more and this is how I'd like to help us do it." You should look at your own life within the church and see how you can better support God's mission. This might be in Sunday

School, Bible Studies, Small Groups, etc. Get involved so that you can grow, but also help others grow at the same time. You were saved by God through Christ, and you've been adopted into a local church family. Spending time with this family is as important and normal as spending Thanksgiving with your biological family.

God's glory abounds in the hearts of His people. This glory is manifest on Earth as His people proclaim Him to the nations and neighbors. Father, what have we done to warrant the trust you have given to us in carrying on this mission? We've done nothing, but receive the redemptive work of Christ by your hand, for your glory.

Study Questions

1. Explain what the mission of God is.
2. How are you actively participating in the mission of God?
3. What can you do to support your church's efforts in carrying out the mission?
4. Why is the mission of God so important?

Use the space that remains to write out what you believe about the mission of God.

God's Law

The Law, which includes the Ten Commandments was given to Israel and then to the church in the New Covenant for a threefold purpose: to expose the holiness of God and sinfulness of man, to restrain evil, and to reveal what is pleasing to God (Ps. 19:7-11, 119:9-16; Rom. 7:7-25, 8:3-4; 1Co. 7:19; Gal. 3:24). The Law, though written on the hearts of men as displayed by their conscience (Rom. 1:21, 2:15, 8:7), is unable to save them. Due to man's fallen nature he is unable to be obedient to the Law. However, the Holy Spirit guides all who believe in Jesus into joyful submission to God, for His glory and their good (Jer. 31:33; Ez. 36:26-27; Heb. 10:16).

Doxology and Application

The most concise yet robust instruction that God gives to His people is the Ten Commandments. The first table, which are the first four commandments, teach us how we relate to God. He is to come first, be worshipped rightly, have reverence for His name, and set aside a day for rest and worship. These are four instructions on how to keep our relationship with God central and how to flourish as His people.

We naturally rebel against God in our fallen state as we seek to replace Him with just about anything that will gratify our flesh. Don't believe me? How often do people skip the gathering of the saints for sports, concerts, or family vacations? When an event comes up on a Sunday morning that would cause us to miss our weekly gathering do we process it through the lens of God's command to worship Him? If we do process it through this lens do we at least groan in our souls as we long to be with God's people as God has designed? Or, do we simply take this aspect of our lives for granted and only participate in the worship of God when it is convenient?—Kind of sounds like idolatry to me. The purpose of the first four commandments is to point us to worship God rightly and reveal our tendency not to.

The second table are commandments five through ten. These commandments teach us how we are to relate to one another. We are to care for and love our parents, treasure all human life, stay faithful in marriage, protect our neighbors' property, be honest in how we speak about others, and be thankful for and content with what we have.

We neglect the call to love our neighbor as yourself (Mark 12:32) when we hear something about them, believe it, then share it with another person before we verify the information. In modern day terms this is slander, in biblical terms it is called bearing false witness. What seems innocuous is actually a sin against our Lord.

His Law reveals His holiness and our sinful inclinations. It restrains evil as the civil authorities legislate and enforce laws. Lastly, it stirs in man through Christ and the Holy Spirit to help us walk in such a way that we glorify God and enjoy Him forever.

The Law points us to the work of Christ. He has fulfilled the Law by obeying it perfectly. Through His death and resurrection, He has imputed to those who believe in Him this perfect righteousness and holiness so that when we break the Law we no longer suffer from its eternal consequences.

Jesus frees us from the bondage of sin, its eternal consequence, and now we can walk humbly behind Christ who fulfilled the Law. When we stumble, God mercifully and by His grace picks us up to continue down His holy path. This is what Paul means when he says to, *"work out your own salvation with fear and trembling"* (Php. 2:12).

We don't serve a God who leaves us without directions, tools, or support. Instead our loving and gracious God directs our paths as the Psalmist records, "*By guarding it according to your word. With my whole heart I seek you; let me not wander from your commandments! I have stored up your word in my heart, that I might not sin against you*" (Ps. 119:10-11).

We are able to walk in such a way because the Holy Spirit indwells us and guides us. When we stumble or are in need of assistance we have been given the church, the people of God to spur us on. We likewise are to spur our fellow believers on.

This is truly a gift from God who loves His people. The Ten Commandments are truly worth praying through, studying, and thanking God for. These words should direct us to the holiness of God in whom we find our greatest joy. He is totally set apart from His creation and unlike anything else in this world.

Study Questions

1. What is the purpose of the Law?
2. How is the Law a blessing to the church?
3. How does Christ free us from the Law?
4. Why has God given us the Law?

Use the space that remains to write out what you believe about God's Law.

The Nature of Man

Man came into existence in Gen. 1:26-2:25 and is made in the image of God. He is given the responsibility of being the manager of all creation. God's formula for man is dust and breath as found in Genesis 2:7. It is in these two parts that man becomes a soul or living being. Apart from the breath of God, man is only dust. Man was created as mortal though he had the opportunity to live in fellowship with God forever in the Garden of Eden. The first man, Adam, forfeited this privilege for all mankind when he rebelled against God (Gen. 3:6-7),God judged Adam's sin by pronouncing the sentence of death (Gen. 2:17) for all of humanity. It is sin that severed the relationship between man and God (James 4:4), resulting in the need for a perfect sacrifice in Jesus to reconcile that relationship. When a man dies, due to man needing two parts to exist as a living person, the breath given to man in Gen. 2:7 returns to God (Eccl. 12:7) until the resurrection, and the body or dust returns to the Earth (Eccl. 12:7).

Doxology and Application

What is man's greatest need in life? The biblical answer is God, which is given to Him in Christ. Man is by his very nature at war with God and rebellious, *"For the mind that is set on the flesh is hostile to God, for it does not submit to God's law; indeed, it cannot"* (Rom. 8:7).

What about the person who seems to be good and kind? Surely they aren't at war with God... —"for all have sinned and fall short of the glory of God" (Rom. 3:23), the Apostle Paul would beg to differ. The fact that sin is at our very core shouldn't be surprising.

In the creation of man we see that he is made in the image of God, *"Let us make man in our image, after our likeness"* (Gen. 1:26). God created man with passion, feeling, wisdom, among other attributes. However, this image and likeness to God was distorted in the fall. When Adam sinned we all sinned so that our nature is like a fuzzy photograph and our image is all pixelated. The restoration of this image begins with the indwelling of the Holy Spirit and redemption accomplished by Jesus Christ. The full restoration will be complete in our glorification until such time God is "conform(ing us) to the image of his Son" (Rom. 8:29).

If we look at the introduction of man in the Bible we see that his first instinct is to lust after that which isn't his. At the fall of Adam we see a man who doesn't protect his wife, allows her to be tricked by Satan, and falls into the same trap. He rejected the very Word of God that he was given when God said, *"You may surely eat of every tree of the garden, but of the tree of the knowledge of good and evil you shall not eat, for in the day that you eat of it you shall surely die."* (Gen. 2:16-17). So what does Adam do? He goes after that which was forbidden by his Creator!

We can find a more contemporary example by observing children. I firmly believe that each child is unique and that their behavior is a mix of nature and nurture, but most children, regardless of upbringing or genetics long for their own toys. Not only do they long for their own toys, but more often than not they are jealous for them. My son might not have played with his Tonka Truck in three years, but if his sister tries to borrow it then his little yellow truck becomes his greatest joy and treasure. He will seek to guard that truck with his life and if his sister successfully "borrows" this precious hunk of metal, then he will do all that is in his power to reclaim it.

My son will use every bit of energy to plot the demise of his sister if she takes one of his toys, even if he hasn't played with it since birth. He will drop whatever activity he was participating in so that he can divert all of his attention on Operation Tonka Grab. A child might never be more motivated or focused than when they are trying to pester their sibling, especially when they are trying to get their property back. This illustrates for us that the human heart above all things is a factory of idols. Selfishness, lust, and idolatry all proceed from our hearts.

This is our life outside of Christ. We continually sin against God due to our lack of belief in Him, *"but whoever does not believe is condemned already, because he has not believed in the name of the only Son of God"* (John 3:18). Due to our unbelief we also constantly violate His law. Sin is our separating of ourselves from God, which results in our death. —*"For the wages of sin is death, but the free gift of God is eternal life in Christ Jesus our Lord"* (Rom. 6:23).

But If sin equals death then Christ equals life! Coming to a biblical understanding of our nature brings to us a great joy in knowing that Christ has saved us. It humbles our minds and hearts to know that, *"We love because he first loved us"* (1 John 4:19). Apart from the work of Christ and our faith in Him then we'd still be in a state that deserves condemnation and destruction. Instead, God, being rich in mercy, *"because of the great love with which he loved us, even when we were dead in our trespasses, made us alive together with Christ"* (Eph. 2:4-5). There is life only in Christ.

A world filled with pestilence, turmoil, and strife — all conditions of a fallen state. These are the afflictions that we have inherited from our first father Adam, but Christ has given us new life by His perfect obedience to your will. Glory be to you for all that we treasure, of which Christ is central.

Study Questions

1. How was man made by God?
2. What is man's greatest problem?
3. When does man begin to rebel against God?
4. How does God plan to redeem man from his sin?

Use the space that remains to write out what you believe about man's nature.

Salvation-Union with Christ

Doctrinal Statement

Union with Christ broadly encompasses all the work of God in our lives: election, calling, regeneration, faith, adoption, justification, and sanctification. These acts of God are applied through man's union with Christ. Jesus had a people set aside for Him by the Father since "before the foundation of the world" (Eph. 1:4). Jesus describes our unity with Him in John 17:23, "I in them and you in me". As Christ and the Father are one and in each other, we are united with Christ.

Doxology and Application

"We stand united" and variations of this phrase are popular in political, national, and organizational movements. When we are trying to express our sense of unity through shared interests, missions, or goals we use these phrases as a way to inculcate and solidify what we believe to be important. By what means are we united together? If you ask this question to 100 people you may very well receive 100 different answers.

If I go to a hockey game, which is a favorite pastime of mine, and I'm wearing a Boston Bruins jersey and ask a fellow spectator "What unites us?", what do you think he might say? You probably want to know what they are wearing, what type of accent they have, and in what city we are partaking of this wondrous sport. A simple answer might be our love of hockey. Another might be our shared affinity for the Bruins, beards, or the state in which we both live. Again, if you ask 100 people this question they all might have different answers. Each of those answers might be acceptable and display for us the diversity of our line of thinking. But what if we asked the same question within a local congregation or a group of local congregations?

In most churches you might get an array of answers. Many have grown up in the same county, attended the same schools and colleges, support the same sports teams, enjoy the same music, etc. These are all good and fine things. They are all true answers that are layers of unity we all share within a local community. But when this becomes the main point of unity within a congregation, the church has lost its way. Why? When a fellow believer moves into the area they will feel less welcome because the points of unity most prominent are things that they are unable to change. More importantly, when these points of unity are most prominent it hides what our most important and foundational point of unity is — Christ.

When we realize that Christ is our greatest point of unity all other layers of unity fall into the background. Within the church we are able to overcome all things because we are united by the One who overcame death. He has united us to Him. Quite literally, He indwells us by the work of the Holy Spirit. It is for this reason that Jesus tells His disciples that it is better for Him to leave so that they would receive the Holy Spirit, God's indwelling presence (John 14:16-17).

Through the Holy Spirit we are united to Christ in His life, death, and resurrection. We have been given His righteousness— it is credited to our account. We have died with Him— we are dead to sin. We have been resurrected with Him— we are raised to an abundant life. Our unity with Christ provides for us an inheritance befitting a King. Through our union with Christ we are also united to one another.

Many churches have experienced great pain through disunity. Chasing after selfish ambition, they lose sight of the fact that they have been given to one another for the mutual edification of their brothers and sisters in Christ. The unity given to the church has been sealed by Christ's death; when we reject this unity with one another we are indeed rejecting our unity with Christ. Sometimes we must leave a church due to unrepentant sin or heresy, but to leave because we don't get our way is an indicator of spiritual immaturity and the reality that our perceived unity wasn't built on Christ to begin with. Instead, our unity was built on our other commonalities, which makes us no different than fans attending a hockey game. Unity that isn't first and foremost based on Christ is worldly, ungodly, and sinful.

May you look to your union with Christ first and foremost as the result of salvation and the means by which you attain God's promises. From this posture of right relationship to God, be encouraged as you engage yourself, the world, and the church as an Ambassador of Christ —one who is united to Him.

In every way you are able to be a minister of reconciliation because you were first reconciled to God through Christ. You bring Christ to others, proclaiming His glory and majesty. You bring those in Christ together when there is strife because their unity is found in Him. You are brought to God by Christ because He has united you to Himself!

Study Questions

1. How are you united to Christ?
2. Why are you united to Christ?
3. What does unity in the local church look like?
4. How can you help defend unity within your local church?

Use the space that remains to write out what you believe about the union with Christ.

Salvation-Calling and Election

Effectual calling and election describes God the Father's choice to save people prior to the foundation of the world. As found in Romans 8:30, "And those whom he predestined he also called," God works all things according to His own will, including those He has chosen for His purposes (Rom. 8:28). With this in mind, there are those who are called who have yet to be saved. There are other aspects of salvation that require a response by an individual, however, the call on an individual to salvation comes solely from God. This effectual call is impossible to resist once one is regenerated and able to respond to God in faith and repentance.

Doxology and Application

Imagine with me a mother who is calling for her young son from her front porch. The family lives in a crowded neighborhood with cars, joggers, bicyclists, and children playing basketball. She calls for her young son as she often does when it is time to come inside for lunch or dinner. The mom has a particular way she pitches her yell, and she already has a unique enough voice that her words cut through the polluted noise of a busy evening. When the words of this patient and loving mother reach the boy he has options. He is able to hear her call and come home, or allow her words to remain muddled in the ambient noise of today's busy neighborhoods.

The call of a mother to her children to come home may be clear, but only if her children are listening. God's call to His people is such that His Words are heard and heeded. The Gospel has a general call to the world like the mother yelling into the neighborhood. God's people hear the call of their Lord and like His sheep they obey their Shepherd. Jesus tells us that, *"the sheep follow him, for they know his voice"* (Jn. 10:4). In fact, a sheep who ignores the Shepherd's call proves himself to not be of the flock. A child from the neighborhood might come to the mother who is yelling for their son, but this alien child won't heed the instruction of the mother to come in for dinner. Why? This child doesn't belong to this mother and will eventually go off back to where they came.

There might be those who come at the call of the Gospel who will never enter into the Kingdom, but once the Shepherd says, *"If anyone would come after me, let him deny himself and take up his cross and follow me"* (Mt. 16:24), the imposter will run away into his own dominion. The call of God is sufficient and irresistible to the ones He calls. The son who hears his mother's voice must return to her. The voice of God is sweeter than all other sounds combined as it calls to His people to abandon their sin, believe in Christ, and receive cleansing from all wrongdoing.

We learn that God chose His people long before His people even existed, *"even as he chose us in him before the foundation of the world, that we should be holy and blameless before him"* (Eph. 1:4). So at the appointed time He makes His voice clear to us to come home where we belong. God's people are called home and the road is paved in the blood of His Son, making the trek possible.

When we enter into the Kingdom He calls us to feast on His Word and gives us the elements of communion as a perpetual heavenly feast. At times when we resist it isn't from a lack of His sufficiency or sovereignty, but our lack of satisfaction in Him. By His grace and mercy He continues His call through the proclamation of the Gospel so that we would increase in our absolute reliance and supreme satisfaction in Him.

Trust in God, my friend, and glorify Him in all things. He knew you before you knew yourself. Prior to your creation in your mother's womb, God knew the number of your days. He knew the moment you would trust in Him and you'd be welcomed into the Kingdom. At that moment there was great rejoicing in heaven as the family of God saw their prodigal come home.

What might this mean in our sharing of the Gospel? We can have absolute confidence that as the Gospel is proclaimed in our homes, communities, and across the world, God is at work. He is working by tilling the soil of the hearers' hearts, planting the seeds of gospel proclamation, and watering with His divine Word. The Word of God will either harden hearts as it did with Pharaoh or soften them as it did with yours. As the heart is softened, seeds of faith are planted and fertilized as the Gospel is proclaimed over and over again in someone's life.

If we trust in the work of God for salvation then we must also trust in His work as we share Him with others. As Jesus taught Nicodemus, *"The wind blows where it wishes, and you hear its sound, but you do not know where it comes from or where it goes. So it is with everyone who is born of the Spirit."* (John 3:8)

The Spirit comes upon a person as they hear the Gospel call and it becomes sweet, clear, and warm, so that they run home as fast as they can. The call of God is comforting to the touch and like an all encompassing embrace between a father and child. Why? Because it is the enveloping of many sons as their Heavenly Father fits them for eternity with their elder brother's clothing— righteousness.

The call of God towards His elect is like the mother calling for her son. He finally hears her through the polluted air of distraction. She has opened his ears like God opens our minds and hearts. He plucks us out of darkness, having adopted us into our family, and makes us aware of the adoption papers that have already been signed. We now step into our new home having shed our old selves and putting on the new.

Study Questions

1. When does God call for His children?
2. Are there any conditions that God puts on His children for Him to call them?
3. What means does God use to call His people?
4. Explain God's sovereignty in His call to people.

Use the space that remains to write out what you believe about calling and election.

Salvation-Atonement

Doctrinal Statement

Penal Substitutionary Atonement includes all of the atoning work of Jesus Christ in His death. It is the New Testament fulfillment of the Old Testament practice of the atoning work of priests and goats. On the Day of Atonement the High Priest would lay his hand upon a goat and transfer the sin of Israel to it. They would then drive the goat, called the scapegoat, out of Israel. The second goat would be slain and his blood laid on the mercy seat of God. This annual event represented the satisfaction of God's wrath towards sin on behalf of Israel. This practice is a foreshadowing of the future perfect atonement in Christ's death (Heb. 10:1-4).

To properly understand this doctrine, we must familiarize ourselves with three terms:

Expiation is the aspect of the atonement that sees the removal of sin from man to the scapegoat. In the New Covenant this is accomplished at man's sin being taken upon Jesus (2 Cor. 5:21). (Ps. 103:12; Isa. 53:5)

Propitiation is the aspect of the atonement that sees the punishment of sin exercised on Jesus, thereby satisfying wrath and justice accomplished.

Particular is a term that we use when describing the atonement that describes the extent of Jesus' work. His atoning sacrifice is sufficient for all but effective for those who are called, elected to salvation, and saved (Jn. 10:14-15; Rev. 22:17; Rom. 8:28-30).

Doxology and Application

The atonement is one of the most important aspects of Christ's work for us to properly understand. It speaks to the depth and breadth of all that is accomplished by Jesus' death. It expresses how deeply we have sinned against God and all that He, in His righteousness, demands in order for justice to be fully realized.

When one says that "Jesus paid the penalty for sin", what do they mean by that? First, they mean that our sin has been transferred to Jesus. This is what Paul means by, *"For our sake he made him to be sin who knew no sin"* (2 Cor. 5:21a). Jesus in Himself has absolutely no sin. In every way Christ is perfect. His perfection and taking on human nature is what makes Him our perfect lamb, which was the requirement in the Old Testament for the atoning sacrifice. Jesus as our High Priest freely transferred our sin to Himself so that His death would satisfy the wrath of God completely.

The next aspect of the atonement is the satisfaction of God's wrath. Due to God's very nature being holy and just, holiness and justice proceed from Him. To say a person is just is to say that they act in a way that is morally and ethically right. To say that God is just is to say something about the nature of justice itself; it is part of His nature and character. God is morally and ethically right in every way. In order for God to fully reconcile His people back to Himself He cleanses them by transferring their sin to Jesus and then crushes Him. His wrath is satisfied fully, *"But he was pierced for our transgressions; he was crushed for our iniquities; upon him was the chastisement that brought us peace, and with his wounds we are healed"* (Isa. 53:5).

One aspect of the atonement that can be overlooked is the willingness of The Son to obey The Father. He was obedient to the point of death (Php. 2:8). He didn't begrudgingly go to the cross, but did so without hesitation or reservation. It was His mission and desire to redeem His people that His Father set aside for Him since before the foundation of the world. Jesus' work was directed by the Father, but not without the Son's willingness.

Now who are the beneficiaries of this work? Those who have been called by God and saved. Continuing our illustration of the mother calling her son to come home, she calls only her son. Others might hear the call to her son, but only the son responds. Only the son who is called by his mother will benefit from her work and care. One would properly refer to this call as particular, effectual, and limited to the one being summoned. The same thing can be said about the call of God and the work of Jesus. The atonement is particular to God's people.

Why is this important? It reminds us that the wrath of God is satisfied for His people, but He still requires the lost to answer for their rebellion. This is accomplished in their destruction at the return of Christ (Jude 1:5, 10).

The atonement is the greatest gift God has ever bestowed upon His people. It is a gift that is perpetual and inexhaustible as it is truly effective in satisfying God's righteous wrath. Unlike the Day of Atonement for the Jews, our Day of Atonement is the day that Jesus died on the cross. We no longer need to offer an annual sacrifice for our sin. Sacrifice has already been made on our behalf and applied fully when we come to faith. The rest of our lives is marked by walking in the work of Christ. We are no longer bound by sin, nor are we subject to its punishment.

This is exceedingly good news! In a world where we tend to punish ourselves for our mistakes and failures and the pain that we cause, we can look to the work of Christ and see that justice has already been meted out. His wrath has been satisfied thereby relieving you of any satisfaction that you think you need to provide. There's no work of man that can satisfy the requirement of God. There's no labor of man more effective than the finished work of God. In the areas of your life in which you find incredible despair you are now able to look to God and see that He offers to you forgiveness and freedom.

Who has any right to hold your sin against you when God is satisfied? The Creator and Sustainer of all things now looks to you and sees the righteousness of Christ (2 Cor. 5:21b). Though you might not feel righteous at times and don't always act on it, the reality is that you are clothed with it. It has been given to you by God and now you can freely walk in the light of Christ. So when you fall short you don't need to dwell on your failings, you should dwell on the expansive love of God in Christ.

Study Questions

1. How do the Old Testament sacrifices point to Jesus' perfect sacrifice?
2. What is the difference between the death of Jesus and the Day of atonement?
3. Why is the atonement good news?
4. How does the atonement affect the way you view yourself and others?

Use the space that remains to write out what you believe about the Atonement.

Salvation- Regeneration

Doctrinal Statement

Regeneration is the act of the Spirit in creating a new heart in an individual who has been called by the Father. We are spiritually dead prior to regeneration (Eph. 2:1-3) but are born again by the Spirit (Jn. 3:7). Man is completely depraved prior to regeneration, unable to come to God on his own. As Jeremiah 17:9 indicates, "The heart is deceitful above all things, and desperately sick". Despite God instructing man to write His law on their hearts (Deut. 6:6), they are unable to do so. It is only God who is able to write the law on man's heart through the work of the Spirit, "I will put my law within them, and I will write it on their hearts." It is by God's grace that the Spirit transforms the nature of an individual so that he is able to respond to God's call in faith and repentance (Col.3:10).

Doxology and Application

In the last chapter we discussed God's calling and election of His people. Regeneration is the action that results from the effect of God's call. To borrow from our previous illustration regarding the mother calling her son, regeneration is the point at which the son's heart changes from rebellion (not wanting to leave his present activities) to obedience. In the next two chapters we will likewise discuss the next steps in the order of salvation— faith and repentance.

Hearts are naturally in a state of rebellion. People are totally incapable of enjoying God and allying themselves fully to His cause. In John chapter 3, Jesus uses an illustration with Nicodemus, a teacher, to explain how one comes into the Kingdom of God. He uses birth for this illustration and calls it being "born again" or "born from above."

"Truly, truly, I say to you, unless one is born again he cannot see the kingdom of God." Nicodemus said to him, "How can a man be born when he is old? Can he enter a second time into his mother's womb and be born?" Jesus answered, "Truly, truly, I say to you, unless one is born of water and the Spirit, he cannot enter the kingdom of God." (John 3:3-5)

Nicodemus asks a very insightful question, which incites a response from Jesus that gives us insight as to how one can truly enter into the grace of God— by God causing Him to be born again. Think of when a child is born. It is a glorious day full of joy as new life enters into the world. Has anyone ever born themselves? Do you know of a child climbing out of her mother's womb on her own accord, under her own power, and by her own will? No, of course not! It is absurd to think that a child wills itself to be born or climbs out of the womb. Such is the case with being born again, it's not something that we will but God wills.

Jesus goes on to say, *"That which is born of the flesh is flesh, and that which is born of the Spirit is spirit... The wind blows where it wishes, and you hear its sound, but you do not know where it comes from or where it goes. So it is with everyone who is born of the Spirit."* (John 3:6-8). Only the Spirit can descend upon a person's heart and change their very nature. Whom will He descend upon and cause to be born again? Those whom God calls and elects. The Spirit is like the wind in that we don't know what direction He will blow, but we know He will do the work that God intends for Him to do.

Scholars and theologians for centuries have discussed the nature of man and his ability to sin and not sin. If we think of Adam prior to the Fall, he had the ability to sin and the ability not to sin. Once Adam rebelled, his nature changed due to his corruption caused by sin. Now man was unable to not sin and able to sin. God provided for Adam and later Israel the ability to atone for their sins through sacrifice, but this sacrifice was limited in its efficacy as Israel awaited the perfect sacrifice of a Savior.

The Holy Spirit in the New Covenant changes the nature of the human heart now giving man the ability to not sin and the ability to sin. When sin occurs we no longer offer a sacrifice, the sacrifice for sin has already been paid on our behalf by Christ. In the New Heaven and New Earth mankind will no longer be subject to sin and fallenness. At this point man will be able to not sin and unable to sin.

For further illustration of how man is changed see the below table from Thomas Boston and inspired by Augustine of Hippo.

Creation	Fall	Redemption	Glory
able to sin	able to sin	able to sin	able to not sin
able to not sin	unable to not sin	able to not sin	unable to sin

Regeneration is God's changing of your nature and being. This is the God you serve,
One who provides for you in every way. He stirs your affections for Him, brings you closer to Him, and changes who you are from the inside out. Now in the

moments of greatest doubt, pain, suffering, and temptation He gives you the ability to flee from despair and take upon the yoke of Christ whose burden is light. Your regenerate heart causes you to mourn over your sin and find joy in forgiveness.

This is one reason why when the Gospel is preached we need not bemoan our unsuccessful attempts at calling people out of their sin and into belief in Christ. Our role is the proclamation of the Gospel to those inside and outside of the faith. God's role is to change hearts and draw people to Himself. You can rest easy when sharing Christ as you rely upon the Spirit to move. He goes where He pleases.

Study Questions

1. What changes when someone's heart is regenerated?
2. Why is someone able to not sin after they are regenerated?
3. How does God empower you to not sin?
4. What happens when you sin with a regenerate heart?
5. Why is this good news?

Use the space that remains to write out what you believe about regeneration.

Salvation-Faith

Doctrinal Statement

Faith is one piece of man's two-part response to God's call and acceptance of His grace, which is referred to as conversion. It is through faith alone that man is saved, not by any work of his own. As Paul writes, "For by grace you have been saved through faith." Saving faith in Jesus is knowledge of who He is, belief in the knowledge of Christ, and trust in Him as Savior (Rom. 10:9). This faith is truly a gift from God. Though it is man's response to God, it is God Himself who provides the faith for the believer to believe (Eph. 2:8-9). Faith is the instrument of salvation by which man is able to receive God's grace.

Doxology and Application

The son in the midst of youthful activities hears the cry of his mother to come home. There is an instant in which the voice of his mother is pleasing and comforting to his ears. He takes a moment and responds positively and runs home as quickly as he can. This boy's response includes the act of faith and belief in which he trusts in his mother's voice, her request to come home, and chooses to act. This is the type of faith exercised at conversion. We have that moment where we trust in our Heavenly Father, believe in our Christ, and trust in Him for salvation.

We already discussed the fact that one is unable to respond positively to the call of God apart from the Holy Spirit regenerating the heart. Likewise, one is unable to have faith in Christ without God giving her that faith. The Apostle Paul writes, *"For by grace you have been saved through faith. And this is not your own doing; it is the gift of God,"* (Eph. 2:8). This faith is a gift from God so that you may believe. You have the ability to choose God once you are regenerated because your nature has been changed. Prior to your regeneration you were unable to choose God because your nature kept you in bondage to sin. The faith that you exercise by trusting in the Lord Jesus Christ for salvation is likewise a gift which God finds great joy in giving.

You might ask yourself why this is the case. Why must faith be given? Can I not exercise faith and belief on my own accord? Why can't I choose to follow Christ on my own? Why must there be an outside force directing me or causing me to believe?

These are all questions that indicate the severity of our self-importance. We are all too prone to making ourselves the heroes of the story. Like the little boy who runs home to his mother we can take pride in our gumption to choose obedience. We reject the notion that our mother has spent years working on us so that one day we may respond with gladness and joy at the sound of her tender voice calling us home to sit with the family for dinner. We made a choice to run home only after our mother took the time and effort by giving us the necessary elements to obey.

Don't take my word for it, salvation is *"not a result of works, so that no one may boast"* (Eph. 2:9). The gift of faith has been bestowed upon God's people because He knows that we are prone to boast in our own accomplishments. If we were to exercise faith on our own accord separate from the work of God and apart from his gift then we'd be quick to lift our nose against the stench of unbelief. We would look at ourselves not as sinners saved by grace, but saints saved by merit. God has given us this gift so that we won't boast. The exact opposite of boasting is humility which causes us to look upon the world with empathy and compassion because we once had no hope; we at one time lacked the faith and trust in Jesus that God has now given to us.

Knowing that faith is a gift reminds us of the hope we have in the proclamation of the Gospel. It is in God's hands to give faith to someone so that they will believe. An increase in faith and trust in Christ is also a gift from God. Jesus tells us to *"ask me anything in my name, I will do it"* (Jn. 14:14), which of course assumes that our asking is in line with the will of God. His will is for us to have faith in Him and trust in Christ.

The gift of faith stokes in our hearts a supreme gratitude towards God. Why did He choose to give us this gift? It's as if we got to read the will of our deceased Aunt Sally and discover that she left us a fortune. You barely knew Aunt Sally and you didn't even particularly like her very much. Why did she decide to give you, of all people, this treasure of riches? She found pleasure in it and now you will spend your life singing the praises of Aunt Sally who out of her benevolent will changed your life forever. You entered into the lawyer's office a beggar and left with endless riches.

After receiving this inheritance you begin to look upon your Aunt Sally with great fondness and express her wondrous deeds to as many that will listen. It took this benevolent gift, which you had no rights over, to truly open your eyes to how great she was. Our God isn't spoken of in the past tense. Instead we are able to proclaim His glory to the world while He is active and watching. We can know that He looks down upon us not only with great joy, but that He is continuing to exercise His will over creation. As you proclaim His name, increase in your knowledge of Him, and worship Him, God takes great joy and is pleased. He's also actively working in your midst by softening hearts and ensuring the Gospel seeds that you are sowing find fertile soil.

Take a moment to consider these words from "How Sweet and Awful Is the Place":

While all our hearts and all our songs
join to admire the feast,
each of us cries, with thankful tongue,
"Lord, why was I a guest?

"Why was I made to hear your voice,
and enter while there's room,
when thousands make a wretched choice,
and rather starve than come?"

'Twas the same love that spread the feast
that sweetly drew us in;
else we had still refused to taste,
and perished in our sin.

Study Questions

1. What is faith?
2. Why does God give you faith?
3. How does this gift change your life?
4. How does this gift change your perception of others?

Use the space that remains to write out what you believe about faith.

Salvation-Repentance

Doctrinal Statement

Repentance is the second part of the two-part response of man to God's call and acceptance of His grace (Mt. 3:2; 4:17). It is through faith alone that man is saved, but repentance and faith are two sides of the same coin. Repentance is feeling sincere sorrow for sin,turning away from sin, and seeking to walk in the ways of the Lord (Ps. 51; Lk. 3:8). If faith is turning to God, repentance is turning away from sin and forsaking it.

Doxology and Application

We return again to our illustration of the mother calling for her son to come home. In the last chapter we looked at the moment in which the son chose to follow his mother's call. In this moment he displays sincere and total trust in the one calling him. What else happens in that moment? He is engrossed in his activities and no matter how harmless they seem to be, they distract and prevent him from going home. As he accepts the call of his mother he also must reject his current endeavor—this decision and action is called repentance.

Repentance is the act in which one turns away from what they are currently doing. To repent of your sin is a necessary component of salvation. How can you run to Christ while still ensnared by your sin? How can the son continue his jaunt around the neighborhood, entertaining himself with the trappings of the world, while also running home to the call of his loving mother? He can't! The boy must turn from his present journey and depart from it so that he can begin anew. That is the exact same thing that happened when you came to Christ. You rejected the things that kept you captive and in bondage. Those chains were released by Christ as you were drawn to Him.

Repentance isn't only something that is reserved for the moment of salvation. That would denigrate the true power of God in your life to nothing more than a "set it and forget it oven". Such a view minimizes your need for God's redemptive work by rejecting that your entire self needs redeeming. It's like making Jesus the frosting on the cake.

Many might think this way. Their lives are built with all kinds of ingredients like hobbies, family, friends, and a career. Jesus is the frosting on the cake that sees you no longer destined for Hell. We call this "Fire Insurance". Here's the thing though-- like a cake, which is delicious, you have some ingredients that affect every aspect of the culinary delight. Without eggs the cake would fall apart. The eggs literally hold everything together and there is no portion that the eggs don't lay claim to. Jesus' redeeming of our lives sees Him lay claim to everything.

This claim of Jesus over our lives is realized when we turn to Him in faith and turn away from the bondage of sin-- leaving our sins behind. For the rest of our lives we will continue to repent and believe. This continued action causes us to gain a greater understanding of Jesus and an ever growing freedom from sin. By this means we realize that our freedoms are truly found in Christ.

Later on we will discuss sanctification, which is marked by our continual repentance from sin. That provides for us a roadmap as to why repentance is important and how it is such a treasured gift from God.

We need help with repentance because it can often be a painful thing when we don't also trust in Christ by faith. Our repentance begins with confronting our fallenness, confessing our sin, and seeking forgiveness.

Confronting sin can be one of the greatest challenges within the Christian life. God blesses us by revealing our sin through His Word. In this moment we consider the ways that we have tricked ourselves into thinking that we have our sin under control and then we confess it to our God. At other times God gifts us with a kind brother who restores us gently.

As Paul writes, *"Brothers, if anyone is caught in any transgression, you who are spiritual should restore him in a spirit of gentleness"* (Gal. 6:1). This brother who restores us is one who truly loves us. If he didn't love us then he'd let us wallow in our sin and see us flounder like a fish out of water or a pig in its filth.

Once confronted with sin we are then called to confess our sin. This should be a confession to the Lord as we lay our burdens at his feet. However, we can also confess our sins to a brother, in fact we ought to. *"Therefore, confess your sins to one another and pray for one another, that you may be healed"* (James 5:16).

For many in the Protestant church we have rejected this practice because of the Roman Catholic connotations that come with it. When we don't confess our sin to one another we miss out on the great opportunity for a fellow believer to pray for us and keep us accountable. God gives us to the church so that we can share in each other's burdens. We are to build one another up, which concludes confession and accountability.

Lastly, we look towards Christ for forgiveness. In fact we are promised this forgiveness through our repentance (Lk. 24:47). Our repentance is part of the forgiveness process. Forgiveness is already available and promised, but our repentance sees us acces that which is already given. In this moment we find supreme joy in knowing that we have been forgiven according to the work of Jesus.

Finally, I'd like to share with you what I find most encouraging about repentance. There are countless times within the life of a Christian that she will be concerned for her own salvation. She might look around and see that her fellow brothers and sisters seem holier and more righteous. They attend Bible Studies more often, have greater knowledge, and seem to have a relationship with God a bit different than her own. This can cause great despair as one is driven not towards the cross, but their own work in earning salvation.

As one is driven from the cross they must take notice of the direction that Satan is steering them. He has taken that which the Lord has purchased and seeks to destroy it. Instead this brother or sister in Christ can look at the tremendous work of God in their life. He hasn't saved them so that they could perform for those around them. Christ has saved them for His good pleasure and glory. Their repentance is all the sign they need in knowing that Christ is at work in their lives. *"Fruit in keeping with repentance"* (Mt. 3:8) is the sign that a believer is no longer in bondage to sin, but completely free in Christ Jesus.

Study Questions

1. What is repentance?
2. How do repentance and faith work together?
3. How is repentance a sign of faith and salvation?
4. Why is repentance important?
5. Who can you confess sin to?

Use the space that remains to write out what you believe about repentance.

Salvation-Justification

Doctrinal Statement

Justification is a legal term that speaks to the legal standing of one who is saved by God. Justification is the declaration of our righteous standing before God. As Paul indicates in Romans 4:5, God justifies the ungodly, through faith and not works. Therefore, one can be declared innocent even though he is guilty (Rom. 3:28). The terms justify and condemn are declarative terms, which simply indicate guilt or innocence. It is Christ's innocence that is imputed to those who are saved (2Co. 5:21).

Doxology and Application

Imagine that you committed a capital offense and stood trial in a court of law. If you are found guilty the imposed punishment is death. The punishment's design is to satisfy justice as demanded by the law. Throughout this trial you hear testimony over and again from countless witnesses attesting to the acts of selfishness and sin that characterize your life.

What kind of terror would be going through your mind as you heard the testimony? Would you regret your actions? Would you mourn over the pain you caused? How might you consider the circumstances that led to such an act befitting such a great punishment? You know that you are guilty, the jury and judge know as well. These witness testimony is overwhelming. The only way to serve justice is to administer the death penalty.

The trial is coming to a close and each lawyer makes their concluding arguments. Your only hope is mercy from the judge. Maybe someone will sympathize and can't bring themselves to see you executed. After a quick deliberation the bailiff walks over to the jury foreman and carries the decision over to the Judge. He asks that everyone stand so that he can read out the verdict that will carry with it your future.

Amazingly, you hear the words, "NOT GUILTY". The crime that you committed has already been accounted for. Someone else was found guilty of the crime even though they didn't physically commit it. That person's innocence is now credited to you as your guilt has been laid on them. This is justification and the one found guilty is Christ. The punishment required by justice has been carried out on your behalf, by

Christ. The Judge now looks at you as completely innocent.

Justification isn't your getting away with murder on a technicality, it's your being found innocent by something outside of yourself. It is an act of God's mercy for sinners by which He no longer considers them sinners, but saints. He no longer counts your sin against you and the punishment is no longer hanging over your head like an anvil waiting to crush you. Jesus has already been crushed and His righteous work accomplished so that you might walk in His life.

This frees us from the bondage of guilt—we no longer must feel that overwhelming feeling for all of the crimes that we have committed. Our past no longer defines us even if it influences us. God sees us no longer as enemies, but family. We have been declared by the Judge as innocent so who else could hold anything against us? The Creator of all things finds no fault in us at our justification. It is a wiping of the slate, making it cleaner than any disinfectant ever could. Paul says, *"For our sake he made him to be sin who knew no sin, so that in him we might become the righteousness of God"* (2 Corin. 5:21).

Our justification frees us from all guilt and unburdens our hearts. A child might grow up to disappoint their parents, but we can never grow up to disappoint our Father in heaven. You might make it a habit of making mistakes in your life that have far reaching consequences or hurt your friends and family. Justification is the application of God's forgiveness so that all our sins and mistakes can no longer haunt us.

You are able to walk out of the courtroom free and clear. As you look around the room and glimpse into the eyes of all those who had heard the testimony and maybe even presumed your guilt, you now see that their perception has changed as well. Not only do they not count your former actions against you, but they praise God for His saving grace. They had committed similar crimes and heard the same verdict. It is why Paul can say, *"From now on, then, we do not know anyone from a worldly perspective... Therefore, if anyone is in Christ, he is a new creation; the old has passed away, and see, the new has come!"* (2 Cor. 5:16-17, CSB)

This new life—free from guilt and shame-- now changes your perspective. Those in your life who are fellow followers of Jesus no longer regard you with disdain for your past, but neither do you regard them in that way. When someone enters into the Kingdom according to God's mercy, His people regard this new brother according to that same mercy given to them in

Christ. That is they look upon this individual as having a new nature and life.

This allows for the dissipation of animosity and the practice of radical forgiveness. When one brother offends another they go to one another and work it out. As one might cause hurt in your life, you are able to go to them and seek their repentance and offer forgiveness. Justification comes by faith alone in Christ alone, and when we rightly understand and apply that justification, our redeemed lives display His inexhaustible grace.

Study Questions

1. What does it mean to be declared righteous?
2. How does justification affect how you see yourself?
3. Why is justification important within the life of the church?
4. Who declares you righteous?
5. Why are you declared righteous?

Use the space that remains to write out what you believe about justification.

Salvation-Adoption

Doctrinal Statement

Adoption is the action and standing of one entering into God's family. Through Christ's work, we are adopted with Him as our brother and his Father as our Father (Jn. 1:12). We become "fellow heirs" with Christ as He becomes not only our Savior but also our brother (Gal. 4:28). This marks a transition as we move out from under the clutches of Satan into the kingdom of God (Eph. 2:2).

Doxology and Application

You've probably heard that friends are the family you choose. No one can help the family they are born into. Each family is unique in its traditions, culture, and values. Some families function smoothly while others might be the epitome of dysfunction. If we are honest, most families have some level of dysfunction, even the ones that are seemingly perfect.

I don't know about you, but I've often heard of the dream family. The family that seemingly has it all together. Mom and Dad are both employed, the kids get along, no one is on drugs, no teenagers get pregnant, and everyone gets along. There's never been a cross word or glance among this mythical group.

When Jesus saves a sinner, He unites them to Himself and they become adopted brothers. Romans 8:29 describes Jesus as, *"the firstborn among many brothers"*. In the previous verse we see that these brothers are saved and are being conformed into the image of their eldest brother, Christ. That means that although one is saved and adopted into this perfect family, they are not perfect themselves. As a family of believers we are collectively being transformed into perfection, but that won't be fully realized until Christ's Second Coming (1 Cor. 13:12).

For this reason, Paul and the other authors of the New Testament offer insight and guidance as to how this family is to live. We are to bear with one another, love one another, and forgive one another. We are to be long-suffering! That means that when we are dysfunctional we are to work tirelessly to overcome our dysfunction. Overcoming this family dysfunction is of course impossible apart from the Holy Spirit.

This is good news to the believer, because prior to this adoption you had been marked for your entire life as a spiritual orphan. Having been adopted into this family you received a far greater Father than your earthly one. You now have God as your Father who knows what is best for you even more than you do. *"And we know that for those who love God all things work together for good, for those who are called according to his purpose"* (Rom. 8:28). As your Father, God is working everything according to His own purposes and pleasure, which is for your good.

There are countless examples of families disbanding for a myriad of sins. There are abusive parents whose children are taken away for their own protection, but God promises that the bruised reed will never be broken in His family (Isa. 42:3). Some might have shortages of food and sustenance, but Jesus says that our every need will be met. In many homes children feel afraid of their father and unable to come to him with any kind of request. That's not the kind of Father we have in God. We are able to go to Him with our every request and our words will be taken to Him by the Holy Spirit.

The family into which God adopts us includes many other brothers and sisters, some who died before we were even born. We are united together as family with the Apostle Paul, Martin Luther, and those around the world who have professed Christ. We are blessed by Calvin's insight handed down from the 16th century and by our neighbor who brings us a meal after we come home from the hospital. We are a family that might have struggles in learning how to get along, but by God's grace He finds no fault in those He calls sons and daughters.

No fault found in those who were the most guilty because the one who had no fault bore our guilt and shame. We've been adopted by the Father into a holy family according to His pleasure and glory. Praise be to God, to Him be the glory forever!

Study Questions

1. What makes God's family so unique?
2. What is adoption?
3. Why does God adopt you?
4. How does adoption change how you view the church?
5. Who adopts you into their family?

Use the space that remains to write out what you believe about adoption.

Salvation-Sanctification

Doctrinal Statement

Sanctification is the process of the saved being set apart and made holy by the work of God. There are two aspects to sanctification: definitive sanctification and progressive sanctification. Definitive sanctification is a one-time event similar to justification in that it is a work of God performed once for all time. It is the movement of a believer into the Kingdom of God from the kingdom of Satan, whereby God sets this person apart for His own purposes (Heb. 9:13-14). This is similar to how God set apart Israel to be His nation. They were set apart by the Law; the church is set apart by the blood of Christ.

Progressive sanctification describes the process of one growing in holiness and righteousness. There is a tension in salvation as one is saved by Christ and is set apart, but they are still subject to temptation in this fallen world until Christ returns (Php. 3:12). The process of sanctification is God's work in us, *"may the God of peace himself sanctify you completely"* (1 Thes. 5:23). This progressive sanctification is what Paul means by "work out your own salvation with fear and trembling" (Php. 2:12). Followers of Jesus are progressively being conformed into the image of Christ (Rom. 8:29), shedding their sinfulness and growing in God's mercy and grace.

As faith and repentance are the response of the regenerate at conversion, so sanctification is the continual response as they walk and grow in faith and repentance. The gifts of faith and repentance aren't only for the new believer, but as one grows in the faith they increasingly rely on Christ in faith and walk away from their sin in repentance.

Doxology and Application

Thinking back to justification, wherein you and I have been declared righteous, we walk out of the courtroom and must now wrestle with our compulsion to commit even more crimes. We have been declared innocent, our nature has been changed, and we are now able to not sin as well as able to sin. Each and every day we will have choices as temptations crash into us like a wave into a tiny skiff. What are we to do?

At the moment of our conversion to Christ we repented of our sin and turned to Jesus in faith. Some mistake this as a one time event, thinking that we no longer need to turn away from our sin because we've already done that. I urge you not to fall into this trap of thinking that faith and repentance are only for the newly converted. Instead, think of faith and repentance as the continual gift from God that washes you in His new mercies each day. What else might Paul mean in Philippians 2:12 when he says, *"as you have always obeyed, so now, not only as in my presence but much more in my absence, work out your own salvation with fear and trembling"*.

Christ has called His people to a life of crucifying their flesh, carrying their crosses, and learning all that He's commanded. This is quite the daunting task when you confuse these calls as being something you must do on your own. Jesus brings much relief to the downtrodden when He says, *"Take my yoke upon you, and learn from me, for I am gentle and lowly in heart, and you will find rest for your souls"* (Mt. 11:29). This life into whichHe brings us is a gift from Him. He purchases our new life His blood, applies that life by the Holy Spirit, and we are spurs us on as His yoke comes around our necks and lifts us up from the despair of our iniquities.

Our continual walk in the ways of The Lord is guided by the Holy Spirit. Jesus says, *"When the Spirit of truth comes, he will guide you into all the truth"* (John 16:13). The Spirit will convict us of our sin—causing us to repent, turn away from sin and sense a sincere sorrow.

The Spirit will also lift us up in faith—causing us to believe in Christ's forgiveness because we know He satisfied the wrath of God and reconciled us to Him. We can trust in God and His work in our lives as He lovingly reveals our inadequacies and iniquities. We can praise Him as He mercifully applies the soothing balm of Christ's work to every crack and crevice of our hearts and lives.

Sanctification is the soothing of our souls as they are pricked by God who reveals our sinful inclinations. He brings us in front of the mirror to confront within ourselves our rebellion against Him. God uses the ups and downs of life— the peaks and valleys-- to demonstrate His love for us as we learn to rely on Him in both feast and famine. The famine causes us to see whether we have realized that God is truly enough in our lives. Famine causes us to discern whether or not Christ is our greatest treasure. The feasts or peaks of life challenge us to not forget our God. Do we continue to treasure Christ and worship Him when we are surrounded by the comforts of this world?

Our lives are forever marked by Christ. Sanctification is God's process of seeing that mark cover our entire body. Think of a man who is balding. Typically his hair begins to thin, spots begin to develop where there is no hair, and at the end of a man's life he could be completely bald or have some sort of bald pattern. This is what sanctification looks like in the life of a believer. God saves you by His grace and mercy, then for the rest of your life that work spreads over your entire being—conforming you into the image of Christ.

This process happens at different rates for different people, but it does happen. You've been set apart by God and now you are continuing to be set apart by His work in your life. As He works you respond by turning from your sin and running towards Christ. Your life is one of continual turning from the world and running into the loving and gracious arms of your Savior. Charles Spurgeon likens it to a ship that is taking off from port. The crew and its captain work together to reach their destination as safely as possible. Factors such as wind, current, and power can all affect the journey. Nevertheless, the journey leads to the destination.

Lastly, you need not compare yourself to others, only to Christ. When Paul writes that *"those whom he foreknew he also predestined to be conformed to the image of his Son"* (Rom. 8:29), he is making a definitive statement about who we are to compare ourselves to. In a world where we are pointed towards airbrushed and photoshopped people as the model of life— God points us to His Son. The world points you to products, diets, and clothes in order to appear closer to their standard of worthiness. God clothes you with the perfection of His Son and empowers you to grow into that perfection. When you struggle with self image and confidence, look towards the Christ revealed to you in the Scriptures. He is perfect and perfectly making you like him

Study Questions

1. What are the two forms of sanctification?
2. Describe sanctification.
3. Why is sanctification a gift?
4. What is the purpose of sanctification?
5. Who receives this gift?

Use the space that remains to write out what you believe about sanctification.

The Second Coming

Doctrinal Statement

Jesus' Second Coming is a promise that He will return to raise the dead, lost and saved alike (Jn. 14:3 Acts 1:11; 1 Cor. 15). It is at this time that Jesus will judge us all according to our deeds and faith (Matt. 25:31-46). The Second Coming is something all believers should look forward to (1 Thes. 4:13-18) but not attempt to predict. Only God knows of the time when Jesus will come back (Matt. 24:26).

The saved will enjoy eternal life with Jesus in the New Heaven and New Earth (Matt. 25:31-46; Rev. 21). As it relates to the Second Coming, eternal refers to the length of time (forever) not the quality. It is at this time that all believers will receive glorified bodies (2 Cor. 5:1-3) to live with God forever.

The Lost will also be raised at the Second Coming of Christ (Matt. 25:31-46). Those who are not in Christ will suffer judgment, condemnation, and eternal (forever) destruction (Matt. 25:46; 2 Thes. 1:8-9).

Doxology and Application

For centuries the theological study of the Second Coming of Christ has sparked tremendous intrigue. Predicting dates was a mistake of many, particularly in 19th century America with the Adventist movement. It's also been a debatable topic as people seek to know when Christ will return in relation to a millennial reign and tribulation mentioned in the book of Revelation. This has caused Christians since the 1st century to believe they are in the last days, and so we are.

One must remember that God doesn't count time like we do, so when we declare that we are in the last days we can be correct without necessarily being literal. Christ calls us to live as though He could return at any moment. Why might that be? When we let go of a promised future on Earth we can more readily embrace God's promised future with Him in the New Heaven and New Earth (Rev. 21).

The realities of Christ's Second Coming are clear in Scripture but some things aren't as easily understood. Why might that be? Apocalyptic literature such as the books of Daniel and Revelation rely heavily on imagery common in the ancient world. Some theologians take an approach to interpretation that is highly literal while others tend towards a more allegorical approach. Then there are those who meet in the middle. Regardless of how one interprets the Apocalyptic books of the Bible there are several things in which we can find agreement and great joy.

A person could read the Gospels and get the impression that the Savior has abandoned His people. In fact this is the sense that the Apostles had when Jesus said He was going away. They responded indignantly as they were told by their Rabbi that not only was He going away, but they weren't allowed to come with Him. Imagine the level of betrayal one would feel after abandoning their entire lives to follow a teacher. Then the teacher says, "Bye guys, I'm going home and you can't come."

The reason that the Apostles couldn't go with Jesus to heaven was for the sake of His mission, of which they were an integral part. They were to *"Go therefore and make disciples of all nations, baptizing them in the name of the Father and of the Son and of the Holy Spirit, teaching them to observe all that I have commanded you"* (Mt. 28:19-20). Jesus even asked the Father in John 17 to keep His followers in the world so that His light and glory would be made manifest in their midst. So although our home is in heaven, God has made us ambassadors to this world with the ministry of reconciliation—that is to administer the reconciling love of Christ and rejoice in fruit that love bears.

Jesus of course tells His disciples that He is going away to prepare a place for them. So when He tells His disciples that they can't come with Him to their heavenly home, He reassures them that He is bringing their home to them. Christ's return will see the ushering in of an eternal Kingdom over which His people will reign with Him forever. Jesus doesn't bring us to heaven, He is bringing heaven to us.

It is at this time that God's people will enjoy Him forever unaffected by the fallenness of the world—because the world will no longer be fallen. It is a time that God's people will no longer be subject to sin—because there will be no more sin. God has saved His people since before the foundation of the world, at Christ's death and at their moment of conversion. The Second Coming is the last bit of salvation to be realized. It is the fulfillment of salvation and all the promises that come with it.

This is very good news to the Christian. We are able to look forward to a time where there will be no evil, sickness, or disease. Everything will be fully restored in the New Heaven and New Earth. No matter what kind of illness or tragedy comes your way today or tomorrow, you can always look towards God and His promise of this perfect future. In this life there is great sorrow and doubt, but when Christ returns we will fully realize the perfection in which we've been clothed. I encourage you to take great comfort in knowing that God has not forgotten His people. He awaits until the appointed time to send the King to reign over His people. The Apostle Peter writes, *"The Lord is not slow to fulfill his promise as some count slowness, but is patient toward you, not wishing that any should perish, but that all should reach repentance"* (2 Pet. 3:9)

Study Questions

1. What is the difference between the destiny of the saved and the lost?
2. Describe what heaven will be like.
3. Why couldn't Jesus' disciples follow Him to heaven?
4. How is the Second Coming the fulfillment of God's promises?

Use the space that remains to write out what you believe about the Second Coming.

Now What?

These truths have been taught since the 1st Century and are immensely valuable today. There is no greater knowledge in life than the knowledge of God. His Word is a gift to us so that we may know Him and rejoice. You and I are called to a lifetime of enjoying salvation through Christ in whom we have been given eternity. Until such a time that our life on Earth ends, we are called to grow in our faith and knowledge of God.

I pray that this has only been a starting point for you and that this will launch you on a journey of further study. There is much to learn and be comforted by. When my mother died unexpectedly, not too long ago, it was the work of Puritan Richard Sibbes who ministered Christ in my great hour of need. When I wasn't quite sure what it meant to be a pastor, Richard Baxter and Charles Spurgeon pointed me in the right direction. At one time I grew weary of self-centered Christianity and David Platt pointed me to the call of making disciples.

There are an infinite number of works by men and women far greater than me that will walk you through the Christian faith. These works are only as effective as they are biblical. I encourage you to take the truths you learned in this work and apply them to your life. Find freedom in justification, rest in the atonement, thankfulness in sanctification, worship in the Trinity, and purpose in the mission of God.

What I covered in this book is only a shadow of what the Bible teaches. Men such as John Calvin, Hermann Bavinck, and Louis Berkhof have works that will give you a lifetime of reading, leading to awe and wonder of God's grandeur and holiness. Take this as a stepping stone into a world in which God unveils Himself and you can see the beauty of your Creator.

Get with some friends in church and read this together. Once you're done, move onto something a bit more challenging (see resources at the back). As you gather together discuss each chapter and doctrine. Iron sharpens iron, so get to work in discussing how these doctrines lead you to a greater love and joy for God. Watch this knowledge turn into praise and then take that to the world in sharing your hope in Christ. You could invite friends that might not yet know Jesus. Be winsome in your conversations and sensitive to their backgrounds. Encourage them to challenge the claims in this book and welcome good dialogue.

Lastly, I have grown quite concerned about the number of well known Christians who share deconversion stories, about how they left the faith. My concern isn't that they left the faith because there will always be those who profess Christ and walk away. They weren't ever really in Christ to begin with. However, their questions that went unanswered are what they claim to be the factors in leading them out of the faith. Almost every single one of these questions could have been satisfactorily answered had they studied the historic doctrines of the faith. The Bible has answers to many of our questions, if we will only ask, seek, and knock. My prayer is that this book will lead you on the quest for answers so that you will find your supreme satisfaction in the God who has revealed Himself in His Word, the Holy Scriptures.

Study Questions

1. Why is studying the Bible important?
2. How should the Bible be studied?
3. What use are works written by saints of old?
4. Will you commit to study with at least one other person? Who?

Use the space that remains to write out a plan on how you can further study God's Word and share that study with others.

Recommended Resources

Introduction to Doctrine and Theology

Concise Theology, J.I. Packer
Everyone's A Theologian, R.C. Sproul
Summary of Christian Doctrine, Louis Berkhof
Blessed Hope Catechism
Heidelberg Catechism

Systematic Theology

Systematic Theology, Louis Berkhof
The Institutes of The Christian Religion, John Calvin
Reformed Dogmatics, Herman Bavinck
Westminster Confession of Faith
The Second London Baptist Confession of Faith

Made in the USA
Middletown, DE
23 September 2021